Jude's Missiles

Prayer Declarations From The Book of Jude

Dr. Darius Ellis James

Flames On The Altar Ministry's
Praying Through The Bible Book Collection

Jude's Missiles: Prayer Declarations from the Book of Jude
by Dr. Darius Ellis James
Published by The Empire Effect Agency™.
2900 Delk Rd. Ste 700 Box 252
Marietta, GA 30067
www.flamesonthealtar.com

First printing, 2022.

Scripture quotations marked NKJV are from the New King James Version of the Bible.

Cover Design, Book Formatting & Interior Design
by The Empire Effect Agency ™
www.theempireeffectagency.com

Introduction

This book is one of the many books from the Flames On The Altar Ministry's Praying Through The Bible Book Collection. This book collection aims to pull out powerful and strategic prayer points based on each book and chapter of the Bible. The goal of Dr. Darius Ellis James through this specific book collection is to create effective prayer resources to help the Body of Christ strategically pray scriptures and cultivate a fervent and intimate prayer life.

Jude's Missiles is a book filled with strategic prayer declarations based upon the Bible verses found in the book of Jude. According to Merriam-Webster, a missile is "an object (such as a weapon) thrown or projected usually so as to strike something at a distance." Therefore, just like a missile, the prayers in this book are a weapon fashioned by the Holy Spirit that is yielded by the Believer to strike the enemy at a distance. The prayer declarations in this book are not just for your present but also for your distant future. Prayer is the only thing that the Believer has that can be launched out into his future to attack the enemy and to destroy the plans of Satan against his life and loved ones.

The book of Jude is one of the shortest books of the Bible, possessing only one chapter. The author of the book of Jude was Jude, one of the brothers of Jesus. Jude opens up his letter with a focus on the common salvation that Believers have through Jesus. He then challenges followers of Christ to earnestly contend for their faith. Jude warned about false teachers who had crept into the church and who were perverting the grace of God.

How to Use This Resource
Read out loud these strategic prayer declarations and declare these prayers with boldness, confidence, and faith knowing that your Father in Heaven hears you and desires to answer your prayers and to deliver you from every wicked snare of the enemy!

"Beloved, while I was very diligent to write to you concerning our common salvation, I found it necessary to write to you exhorting you to contend earnestly for the faith which was once for all delivered to the saints."

Jude 1:3

Prayer
Declarations

Jude 1:1

Based on Verse 1

"Jude, a bondservant of Jesus Christ, and brother of James, to those who are called, sanctified by God the Father, and preserved in Jesus Christ:" **- Jude 1:1**

Prayer Declaration:

Lord Jesus, make me your faithful servant for all of the days of my life! Holy Ghost, sanctify me. Sanctify my mind, my heart, my body, and my emotions. Lord Jesus, preserve my life, keep me in your will, and grace me to answer your call. In Jesus' name, I pray. Amen.

Jude 1:2

Based on Verse 2

"Mercy, peace, and love be multiplied to you." - **Jude 1:2**

Prayer Declaration:

Lord Jesus, multiply my experience of your mercy, your peace, and your love in my life. I silence the enemies of my peace. I rebuke every wall that blocks the flow of God's mercy, peace, and love into my heart and mind. By the grace of God, I declare that I am spiritually aware of the divine mercy, peace, and love of God upon my life. In Jesus' name, I pray. Amen.

Jude 1:3

Based on Verses 3

"Beloved, while I was very diligent to write to you concerning our common salvation, I found it necessary to write to you exhorting you to contend earnestly for the faith which was once for all delivered to the saints." - **Jude 1:3**

Prayer Declaration:

Lord Jesus, give me a desire to contend and to fight for my faith. Give me boldness to preach, give me boldness to testify, give me boldness to evangelize, give me boldness to stand for truth. In Jesus' name, I pray. Amen.

Jude 1:4

Based on Verses 4

"For certain men have crept in unnoticed, who long ago were marked out for this condemnation, ungodly men, who turn the grace of our God into lewdness and deny the only Lord God and our Lord Jesus Christ." **- Jude 1:4**

Prayer Declaration:

Lord Jesus, through the revealing by the Spirit of Truth, exposed every false teacher in my life, every false friend, and every agent of darkness that has been sent to destroy my walk of faith. By discernment through the Holy Ghost, reveal unto me those who have been demonically assigned to my life to bring condemnation, ungodliness, and perversion. Lord, deliver me from the wicked plans of the enemy and open up my spiritual eyes to see every demon, agent of darkness, and demonic plan at work that is trying to go unnoticed. I declare that I see you in the name of Jesus, and I rebuke you! In Jesus' name, I pray. Amen.

Jude 1:5

Based on Verse 5

"But I want to remind you, though you once knew this, that the Lord, having saved the people out of the land of Egypt, afterward destroyed those who did not believe."
 - Jude 1:5

Prayer Declaration:

Lord Jesus, deliver me from the oppression of Egypt. Deliver me from demonic oppression, witchcraft, demonic covenants, familiar spirits, generational curses, and tormenting spirits. Cause your fire to destroy the demons that seek to destroy my life, my destiny, and my family now in the name of Jesus! In Jesus' name, I pray. Amen.

Jude 1:6

Based on Verse 6

"And the angels who did not keep their proper domain, but left their own abode, He has reserved in everlasting chains under darkness for the judgment of the great day;" – **Jude 1:6**

Prayer Declaration:

Lord Jesus, may every familiar spirit, every power of darkness, every agent of darkness, and every principality that wants to destroy my church, my health, my family, my ministry, my children, my marriage, my love for God, my faith, my finances, my business, my education, my health, and my peace be broken now! May those wicked spirits be broken now! May those spirits be destroyed now! May their diabolic plans be aborted now! May they be wrapped in everlasting chains and be sent back to hell now in the mighty name of Jesus! In Jesus' name, I pray. Amen.

Jude 1:7

Based on Verse 7

"as Sodom and Gomorrah, and the cities around them in a similar manner to these, having given themselves over to sexual immorality and gone after strange flesh, are set forth as an example, suffering the vengeance of eternal fire." - **Jude 1:7**

Prayer Declaration:

Lord Jesus, preserve my way. May I not be overtaken by sexual immorality and sexual perversion of any kind. Purify my mind and heart. Make me a standard of holiness, purity, and righteousness in my generation. May I be a reference point for others to say, "I personally know someone who walks like Jesus." May my heart and intentions be purified by the fire of God, and may I have dominion over my fleshly desires. I declare that I am a person of sexual purity in my thoughts and actions. I declare that I walk in the revelation of the pleasure of your presence, and I will delight myself in your word. In Jesus' name, I pray. Amen.

Jude 1:8

Based on Verse 8

*"Likewise also these dreamers defile the flesh, reject authority, and speak evil of dignitaries." - **Jude 1:8***

Prayer Declaration:

Lord Jesus, I shoot forth your arrow of deliverance to strike the enemy and to destroy every friendship, partnership, and association with people who would corrupt my character, the character of my spouse, and the character of my children. Let the defilement of flesh, rejection of authority, and evil speech of leaders never be mentioned about myself and my family. Lord, grace us to live above reproach and help us to resist the temptations of the enemy. In Jesus' name, I pray. Amen.

Jude 1:9

Based on Verse 9

*"Yet Michael the archangel, in contending with the devil, when he disputed about the body of Moses, dared not bring against him a reviling accusation, but said, "The Lord rebuke you!"" - **Jude 1:9***

Prayer Declaration:

Lord Jesus, I release your warring angels to fight on my behalf today against the forces of darkness! I release your warring angels to fight on behalf of my spouse, family, children, business, education, health, ministry, and destiny! I declare that the devil is defeated by the word of God! I proclaim in boldness to Satan and every demon fighting against my destiny and my family's destiny that "The Lord rebuke you!" I am a child of God, a son under authority. Therefore, I operate in authority, and I take authority over every argument of the devil, and I declare that every enemy must be silenced and scattered by the word of God! In Jesus' name, I pray. Amen.

Jude 1:10

Based on Verse 10

"But these speak evil of whatever they do not know; and whatever they know naturally, like brute beasts, in these things they corrupt themselves." - Jude 1:10

Prayer Declaration:

Lord Jesus, I rebuke the evil spoken against my family and myself because of my obedience to you. I destroy and cancel every word curse spoken against my family and myself through the ignorance of others not understanding what you're doing in our lives and because of their own corrupt thoughts about the things of God, my family, my ministry, my career, my business, my education, my health, and myself. In Jesus' name, I pray. Amen.

Jude 1:11

Based on Verse 11

*"Woe to them! For they have gone in the way of Cain, have run greedily in the error of Balaam for profit, and perished in the rebellion of Korah." - **Jude 1:11***

Prayer Declaration:

Lord Jesus, deliver me and my household from the hands of wicked men. Cause our enemies to not triumph over us! Cause us to be favored even by our enemies. Let the words of our mouth and the love of God that we display cause wicked men and women to repent. In the mighty name of Jesus! In Jesus' name, I pray. Amen.

Jude 1:12-13

Based on Verse 12-13

"These are spots in your love feasts, while they feast with you without fear, serving only themselves. They are clouds without water, carried about by the winds; late autumn trees without fruit, twice dead, pulled up by the roots; raging waves of the sea, foaming up their own shame; wandering stars for whom is reserved the blackness of darkness forever." **- Jude 1:12-13**

Prayer Declaration:

Lord Jesus, remove every spot from my love feasts. Let the contamination of the enemy be cleansed out of my house, my life, my children, my spouse, my bloodline, my church, my ministry, my children's education, and my business. Lord, surround me with people who do not seek to just serve themselves. Give me wisdom on how to navigate my dealings with such men and women that are set out to bring corruption and perversion in the church and in the lives of others! May their assignment from the pit of hell not prosper against God's people! In Jesus' name, I pray. Amen.

Jude 1:14-15

Based on Verses 14-15

"Now Enoch, the seventh from Adam, prophesied about these men also, saying, "Behold, the Lord comes with ten thousands of His saints, to execute judgment on all, to convict all who are ungodly among them of all their ungodly deeds which they have committed in an ungodly way, and of all the harsh things which ungodly sinners have spoken against Him."" **- Jude 1:14-15**

Prayer Declaration:

Lord Jesus, arise and may all of your enemies be scattered! May the judgment of God judge every wicked scheme and plot of the enemy against the bride of Christ. Lord, you execute your judgment against all of your enemies. Therefore, let every demon assigned to bring any wicked plan into effect in my life, my family, and in the body of Christ be scattered by the fire of God! In Jesus' name, I pray. Amen.

Jude 1:16-19

Based on Verse 16-19

"These are grumblers, complainers, walking according to their own lusts; and they mouth great swelling words, flattering people to gain advantage. But you, beloved, remember the words which were spoken before by the apostles of our Lord Jesus Christ: how they told you that there would be mockers in the last time who would walk according to their own ungodly lusts. These are sensual persons, who cause divisions, not having the Spirit."
 - Jude 1:16-19

Prayer Declaration:

Lord Jesus, may I not be swept into deception and sin by men and women who walk in the fulfillment of their fleshly desires. May I contend for the faith within me to not be perverted by the old habits of my past and the ungodly lifestyle of others. May I speak and believe the opposite of grumblings, complaints, and lustful desires. May I not be at awe of the demonic flattery of people that are seeking to gain control over me. May your holy word continually be in my heart and brought to my remembrance. Father, where the enemy seeks to bring divisions, I speak unity and fortification by the Spirit of the Living God! In Jesus' name, I pray. Amen.

Jude 1:20-21

Based on Verses 20-21

"But you, beloved, building yourselves up on your most holy faith, praying in the Holy Spirit, keep yourselves in the love of God, looking for the mercy of our Lord Jesus Christ unto eternal life." **- Jude 1:20-21**

Prayer Declaration:

Lord Jesus, grace me to build my faith through the power of the Holy Ghost, through prayer, and through your word. Let the anointing of intercession fall upon me that I may pray with fervency and longevity! Increase my capacity for prayer! Baptize me in your precious Holy Spirit and make me your house of prayer! Help my unbelief, oh God! Help me to meditate on your great love towards me and your new mercies that you release to me every morning. In Jesus' name, I pray. Amen.

Jude 1:22-23

Based on Verse 22-23

"*And on some have compassion, making a distinction; but others save with fear, pulling them out of the fire, hating even the garment defiled by the flesh.*" - **Jude 1:22-23**

Prayer Declaration:

Lord Jesus, give me the wisdom to win souls. By the wisdom and power of the Holy Spirit, Lord, Fill my mouth with your words. May I speak prophetic utterances with boldness! May I preach the Gospel with love and reverence, may my heart be broken over lost souls, and may I respond in obedience to the voice of the Lord. In Jesus' name, I pray. Amen.

Jude 1:24-25

Based on Verses 24-25

*"Now to Him who is able to keep you from stumbling, and to present you faultless before the presence of His glory with exceeding joy, To God our Savior, who alone is wise, be glory and majesty, dominion and power, both now and forever. Amen." - **Jude 1:24-25**

Prayer Declaration:

Lord Jesus, only you can keep me from falling. So, I ask you, Lord, to keep me. Only you can present me faultless before the presence of your glory with exceeding joy. So, I ask that your blood would wash me now and that you would purify me from all unrighteousness. May I live to glorify you, to know you deeply, to love you, and to praise your name. In Jesus' name, I pray. Amen.

About the Author

Minister Darius Ellis James, EdD, MPH is the founder and executive director of Flames On The Altar, a prayer ministry that exists to provoke every generation to prayer. Dr. James desires to see people, young and old, live a lifestyle of passionate devotion to God through prayer. The purpose of Flames On The Altar is to eliminate prayerlessness, increase people's hunger and thirst for God's word and presence, and empower people to walk boldly in their identity as a son and daughter of God.

Darius has several years of experience in both high school and college ministry. Darius is a leader in tech non-profit and a former high school teacher. He deeply believes in investing in the next generation. He is the author of a 50-day prayer devotional for fathers called *Legend: A Father's Prayers For His Son.* The book addresses 50 topics with guided prayers and scriptures that fathers can use as they learn how to develop a consistent prayer life and the discipline of covering their family in prayer. Darius is also the author of several other books: *God's Ink - A Collection of Faith-Based Poems, God's Daughters - A Practical Guide For Praying For Your Daughter,* and many more that are in the works.

Darius was raised between two small, historic towns, Notasulga and Tuskegee, Alabama; he is the husband of Ebony D. James and the father of two boys, Legend and Conquer.

Resources & Apparel

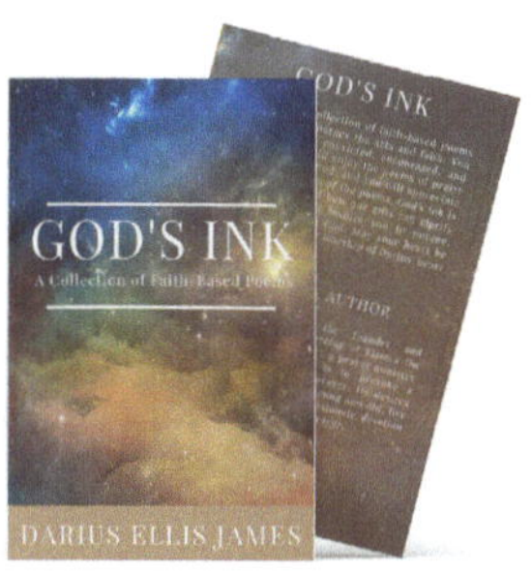

Order Your Shirt(s) Today at

www.flamesonthealtar.com